The Little Blue Horse

Story by Susan D. Price   Illustrations by Sharyn Madder

Clare was Abby's best friend. When she went to Abby's house, they always played with Abby's toy horses.

Clare and Abby
would make the horses
go across the table
and jump over little fences.

The horse that Abby liked best
was a little blue one
with a long white tail.

Abby was always careful
when she played with it.
She didn't want her best horse
to get broken.

But one day, the little blue horse slipped out of Clare's hand, and a leg broke off.

Clare looked down
at the little blue horse.
She started to cry.

"Don't cry, Clare," said Abby's mom.
"I can glue the leg on again."

Clare and Abby watched
as Mom tried to fix the horse.

"Soon your horse
will be as good as new,"
said Mom.

Fix-it
Glue

But when the glue was dry,
the little blue horse
kept falling over.

They could not get the blue horse to stay on its feet.

Clare and Abby were very sad.

The next Saturday,
Clare was in town with her dad.
They stopped to look
in a store window.

Clare could see a lot of old things.
She saw some old teddy bears
and some old books.

Nothing New
SALE
SALE

And then Clare saw
a little blue horse
with a long white tail.
It was just like the one
she had broken.

"Dad, look at that little horse!"
cried Clare.
"I have to buy it for Abby."

Nothing New
SALE

Clare took her money
out of her pocket
and looked at it.

"Do you want me to come in
with you?" asked Dad.

"No thanks," said Clare.
"I want to buy it all by myself."

And she went into the store.

Not

Then Dad took Clare to Abby's house.
"Look, Abby!" said Clare.
"Look what I found in a store!"

"A little blue horse!" laughed Abby.
"It's just like my other one.
Oh **thank** you, Clare!"